Might F*ck off to Australia…

The answers to the questions you have about moving to Australia with a working holiday visa.

By

Carly Murden

Dedicated to Jenna and all the people that asked me questions.

Table of Contents

The more spontaneous you live your life, the better quality it will be, regardless of how much money you have - Bunker Spreckels

Introduction

I have winged it every step of the way while living and working in Australia. From buying the plane ticket to setting up where to live, work, etc.... I originally intended to go for two months to attend a wedding. However, due to my increasing "winging it" skills, I have lived here for over a year and a half now. And it is the greatest thing that has ever happened for me.

It could be one of the greatest things that happen for you too.

I have growing expertise on the common questions you have about moving to Australia with a working holiday visa. My goal for you is that you finish this book feeling knowledgeable, prepared, and excited to go to, what I believe, one of the most amazing countries on Earth. After reading, I want you to feel the freedom to wing it more on your terms, not in the "technical" aspects.

Whatever your interests are in this world, I promise you Australia has it!

So, if you are contemplating f*cking off to Australia, then this book is the one for you. I am the solution to your problems. I set you up for success by getting straight to the point and give you specific details that you cannot find in other places. Each chapter answers a question or "thought" you may have about going to Oz, as well as additional resources, worksheets, and links.

Whoever you are, I am very excited for you!

Thought #1: I can't go to Australia because it's too expensive.

Have you ever been told, something along the lines of: "It's really expensive over there... good luck."

Well, I sure as hell didn't think it was going to be for free.

Cars are expensive, houses are expensive, clothes are expensive... Why is it when we think of a place being "too expensive" it is a reason not to go?

Yet, in reality, you are surrounded by these expenses all the time.

If someone tells you Australia is "too expensive" to travel to or live in as a reason for you to not go, please follow this easy three step process:

Step 1: Look at them in the eye, hopefully you are wearing big sunnies for a stronger effect, and reply with: "Oh, really?"

Step 2: Direct them to Amazon and have them purchase "Might F*ck off to Australia..." for their own evidential matters.

Step 3: Tell them to, "piss off mate!"and make sure you keep their contact information, so you can send them a picture of you living your best life under the Australian sun.

I lived on the couch at my uncle's house for five months…

Was it lonely? Yes.
Was it hard? Yes.
Was it a hard couch? Yes.

But it got me to Australia.

For f*ck sake, if I can do it, you can.

Australia Saving Plan

If you are living in the United States, go to scottscheapflights.com and sign up to be on their free email list if you are not already. Do it right now! It takes two seconds.

Scott and his team send out email alerts whenever they find super cheap flights to random places in the world from airports throughout the US. I bought my round-trip ticket from North Carolina to Sydney for $670 USD... WTF!!!

Even if you are not based in the states, still sign up, you could find a cheap flight to a major city from where you are based that has an email alert.

This plan is made for you to visualise what you are saving for and extra ways for you to make that possible.

Writing down the items that you specifically want to have money for will help you see the bigger picture of your overall Australia Saving Goal. Even though you may not fully know what you are going to do or where you are going to be living yet, write down all of the things you know or think you want to do when you land in Oz.

Make sure you write down anything that comes to mind. It could be the smallest thing such as eating Australian snacks or cuddling a koala. Or larger things, such as going on a dive trip or renting a van to travel the coast. Anything and everything, write it down.

Now that you have your list, which hopefully is a very long one, you are going to put each item into one of these five categories:

1. **Food** (groceries, restaurants, snacks, alcohol)
2. **Transportation** (bus, airfare, Uber rides, buying a car)
3. **Accommodation** (weekly rent, hostels, Airbnb's, hotels)
4. **Entertainment** (concerts, activities, experiences)

5. **Emergency** (travel insurance, a cushion for if things get tough - you decide what that cushion will be).

   Use the list below to give yourself an idea of how much money you would like to save in each category. Each item has the average price in Australian Dollars (AUD).

Eating out for lunch or dinner	$20 - $40	Hostel per Night	$20
Local Bus Ride	$3	Cigarettes	$25
Plane Ticket inside Australia	$90 - $400	Car	$5,000 - $15,000
Pint of Beer	$8 - $12	Car Insurance	$80/month
Weekly Rent	$200	Cocktail	$12 - $18
Monthly Cell Phone Prepaid Data Plan	$30		

The four important factors that you also need to take note of as you edit your category totals are:

Length of stay. Obviously, it's okay if you do not know. I came thinking I was staying for two months... It's almost been two years.

Your own personal spending habits. You know yourself better than anyone else. Be honest.

Real emergencies. You never know what could happen. Whatever happens (hopefully nothing will), you need to be prepared.

You will be working. Having the work holiday visa is what will help you do everything you have written on your list. However, it is important to not solely rely on the income you think you will have while saving for your move because you just don't know what it will be yet.

Now, add each of your categories together. This number is now your Australia Saving Goal.

Food $_____.

Transportation $_____.

Accommodation $_____.

Entertainment $_____.

Emergency $_____.

My Australia Savings Goal is: _____!

How am I going to save this amount of money?

- *Make a promise to yourself that you will cut out a spending habit you have.*

 Whether that be purchasing a snack at the convenience store when you have food at home or purchasing a drink other than water at a restaurant or buying new clothes when you know you already have a dazzling wardrobe. Put the money that you would have spent towards your Australia Savings each week. It may be hard at first, but the more you practice, the more excited you will feel about saving.

Start with one habit and then slowly move on to others. You will be surprised how much money you spend on little disposable things that will save you in the long run.

- *Create an automatic saving transfer on your bank account.*

Analyse each of your category totals. Come up with a number that you feel good about saving weekly or, better yet daily. If you save $10 every week for six months you will have roughly $260. If you save $10 every day for six months that will give you roughly $1,800 right there.

Setting up an automatic transfer into a savings account through your bank will make this a lot easier and simpler for you. You won't even think about it, you will just know that you have money constantly set aside.

- *Limit yourself to going out to eat only once a week if you must at all.*

I am not saying give up your social life. But, this is a huge money-saving area. Everything about going out to eat adds up over time. Think about how much you would save from tipping alone!

Invite friends over to your home for dinner instead of eating at a restaurant. Try out new recipes for them that you could potentially make yourself in Australia. You are going to need to cook for yourself whether that is on the go, in your new home, or a hostel, so, why not start practicing or getting creative before you leave?

Alcohol is included in this too. Think about it... would you rather have that same old beer at the same old bar, or would you rather have that money for a new beer at a new bar in Australia?

- *Create an extra source of income in some way, somehow.*

You can cut back on expenses and save all you want, but the main way to increase funds is, well, work more and bring in more money!

It always sounds harder than it is, but you can do it. Whether that is walking dogs, cleaning houses, bartending... You have skills. So, use them. Think outside the box and think about how they can bring in extra income on top of what you already do for a living.

The possibilities are endless.

I do not recommend spending a ton of money on unnecessary things to buy for your trip. The majority of the time you will pack too many clothes, too many shoes, too many gadgets... Keep it simple. If you don't use it at home, I can tell you for a fact that you will not use it in Australia. So, save the overpacking and keep your money towards your Australia fund.

If you use the word "might" as in: "I might need these shorts" or "I might need that snazzy fanny-pack," then about 99.99% of the time you are not going to use it.

Go online and print out a picture of one place in Australia that you want to go to. Tape it in your wallet, on the back of your credit card, or in your car. It will remind you of what you are working and saving for.

Having a nice cushion of cash saved before you enter Australia will always feel nicer and more secure than not. If you don't, don't sweat it. I came to Australia on a whim with $4,000. If Australia was skyrocketing expensive, do you think I would have lasted? Probably not. Where there is a will, there is a way. If Australia is on your mind, you will find a way to get there, despite what anyone tells you about the prices.

The magic ingredient for you is the work holiday visa.

Thought #2: How do I get a work visa? What even is a working holiday visa?

There are steps to take to obtain a working holiday visa. The most important thing to know is how to give the best "coo - wee" call. Immigration says you either pass or fail, so get practicing.

The working holiday visa is a gift from the Australian government to the rest of the world… A gateway to endless opportunities and experiences awaiting for you. If Australia is somewhere you have always wanted to be, it could be a missed opportunity if you don't take action by applying for the visa.

A working holiday visa grants you the ability to work and travel around Australia for one year. There are two different kinds of working holiday visas: a 417 and a 462. These numbers are purely categorised for where you are from. They may look and sound confusing, but the primary difference is that some countries require more documents than others.

You can apply for a visa from the ages of 18 through 30 years old. The only people that are exempted from this are Irish, Canadian and French citizens; the age limit is 35.

Australia seems to be a "bucket list" destination, for obvious reasons! However, what is the percentage of people on this Earth that check that box off? If you are 18 - 30 years old, this is the time to go. Think about it... having an opportunity to live, work, travel, and have a gateway of new unknown opportunities in a place that you have a desire to go to? That is a pretty special thing to be offered in this world that does have a time limit.

You can work for one employer for up to six months. Therefore, you could work two different jobs for six months each. With certain requirements, you can extend for a second year working holiday visa: you can learn more about this in Thought #10.

You can apply for your working holiday visa up to a year in advance before you plan on entering Australia. The visa starts when you enter the country. I was granted my visa on January 20, 2019 but I entered the country on February 17, 2019. My visa would then expire February 17, 2020; not January 20, 2020.

The government says most applications are processed within approximately 40 days. It does vary, I suggest that you apply for it at least four months in advance before you plan your trip.

Just like ripping off a band-aid, apply for the visa. I know it is one of those kinds of tasks that people like to put off. You will feel so much better once you apply and it will only take you roughly an hour to fill out the application.

When applying, you will be prompted to create an "immi account." This is the government's website where you will access your visa information. Once submitted, log on to the website to check the status of your application roughly once every other week. I didn't receive an email that it had been granted, so it is important to check up on the status.

With the first year of working holiday visas, you must be outside Australia when the visa is granted.

There are documents and steps you will need to obtain your visa. The 462 Visa requires two extra documents than the 417 visa. You can find what you need on the Visa Checklist.

The current cost of the visa is $485 AUD.

Remember, going to Australia is an investment for your life!

Think of the work holiday visa as a "one size fits all" kind of visa. Its primary purpose is to allow you to work and travel freely. There is a long list of other types of visas including study and skilled visas. If the work holiday visa does not sound like the best fit for you, you can explore more of the visas found on the resource page.

It is important to stay up to date with current travel restrictions and/or changing requirements. This book is a foundation for your future endeavors. However, it is important to stay updated on changes due to external factors.

What Visa am I?

417

Belgium	Canada	Republic of Cyprus	Denmark
Estonia	Finland	France	Germany
Hong Kong	Ireland	Italy	Japan
Korea	Malta	Netherlands	Norway
Sweden	Taiwan	United Kingdom	

462

Argentina	Austria	Chile	China
Czech Republic	Ecuador	Greece	Hungary
Indonesia	Israel	Luxembourg	Malaysia
Peru	Poland	Portugal	San Marino
Singapore	Slovak Republic	Slovenia	Spain
Thailand	Turkey	Uruguay	United States
Vietnam			

Visa Checklist

417 and 462

- **Copy of Passport.** If you do not have a scanner, you can take a picture of it on your phone and save it as a document to upload. I do suggest going to your local library and using their scanner or use a friend's scanner to have a couple of copies of your passport to take with you to Australia.

- **Bank Statement.** You need to have the equivalence of $5000 AUD in your bank account when applying. Simply log on to your bank website and download your recent statement or take a screenshot of it.

- **Two Passport photos.** Hop on over to the post office and have them take your picture. Sign your full name on the back in black ink. Proceed just like with copy of the passport. Take these with you to Australia, they are good to have with you just in case.

Only 462

- **Evidence of Education.** Take a picture or scan a diploma of your secondary/high school education.

- **Evidence of English.** This is for people applying from countries other than New Zealand, Ireland, The United States, The United Kingdom, or Canada. A document related to school or work revolving around English.

Working Holiday Visa Application Party!

When are you going to Oz? If you are not exactly sure when you are going yet, use the time in which you would like to go. Subtract four months from that date. This will be the day you apply for your visa.

What you need:

1. A cup of tea… Or spice it up a bit with an espresso martini!

2. Your documents listed on the checklist.

3. This playlist playing in the background, <u>Australian Working Holiday Visa Application Party</u>, on Spotify.

4. Focus: fill out everything correctly.

5. Commitment: to the submit button.

6. Write in the notes on your phone the day you submitted your application, your password and username for your immi account.

7. Give yourself huge cheers and now commence with a dance party.

Woohoo!

Resources

Working Holiday Visa 417 Application	https://immi.homeaffairs.gov.au/visas/getting-a-visa/visa-listing/work-holiday-417/first-working-holiday-417
Working Holiday Visa 462 Application	https://immi.homeaffairs.gov.au/visas/getting-a-visa/visa-listing/work-holiday-462/first-work-holiday-462
Working Holiday Visa 417 Requirements	https://immi.homeaffairs.gov.au/visas/getting-a-visa/visa-listing/work-holiday-417/first-working-holiday-417#Eligibility
Working Holiday Visa 462 Requirements	https://immi.homeaffairs.gov.au/visas/getting-a-visa/visa-listing/work-holiday-462/first-work-holiday-462#Eligibility

Other visas list	https://immi.homeaffairs.gov.au/visas/getting-a-visa/visa-listing

Thought #3: I am going to be lonely.

News Flash!!! Read all about it: Loneliness can be felt anywhere. It can be felt in your group of friends back home and it can be felt in a cafe sitting by yourself in Australia. It can be anywhere you go. Yeah, it can suck... but it should not be your excuse to miss out on seeing and experiencing new things.

Yes, you will feel lonely at times. But here's another news flash: there are endless amounts of people that are in your same boat and you are not alone in how you are feeling. I know it is hard to remember that in the midst of it all but engrave it into your mind. You are going to meet so many people. People that are going to make you so happy. The kind of people who will open your eyes to so many new and wonderful things! People that will make you laugh, cry (go ahead, roll your eyes...) and see the world in different ways.

I'll talk to ya if you really want to talk to somebody, I am not a trained psychologist or therapist, but what I can be, is a friend.

Your friends and family back home are only a WhatsApp message or FaceTime away. They will be excited to hear from you as much as you are excited to talk to them.

The thoughts of: "I want to go work and travel around Oz, but only if someone goes with me," holds you back. Going alone forces you to talk to people, to step out of your comfort zone, and to have no choice but to figure it out on your own. Which you will learn great skills from. However, if you have the opportunity to have someone go with you and they are on the same wave lengths about what you want to do, then you are also pretty lucky. Just don't ever let someone else turn you away from going to a place you've always wanted to go to.

Besides the plan of meeting up with my friend, Jenna to attend a wedding, (and JetStar cancelling her flight…) I came on my own. In hindsight, if I had applied for the visa with someone else, I don't think I would have gotten to where I am today. And luckily Jenna still made it, even if it was a month later. Would it be nice to experience your Australian life with someone else you know? Yes... Duh! But, I am grateful it didn't really work out that way for me. Maybe it could be that way for you too.

It does not get much lonelier than when you are super hungover by yourself. If you find yourself in this state in Australia, which, let's be honest, you probably will...

1. **Look in the mirror and try to smile to get yourself together. You have to accept that you are responsible for the copious amounts of alcohol you drank and that you cannot blame anyone but yourself. I promise you will bounce back quicker if you have these thoughts.**

2. **Pour yourself a large glass of water and drop a Berocca tablet in. It is full of electrolytes and will bring you back to life.**

3. **As much as you don't feel like it, go for a walk outside to have at least some kind of human interaction. Jumping in the ocean will help too.**

After you have done these three items, you can hopefully have a happier day as well as not feel like you need to leave Australia because of whatever you do or don't remember.

If depression and/or anxiety are things in your world, well I know that the loneliness thought may be on your mind. The important factor to note is that it is going to be very important for you to find a connection wherever you are and wherever you go.

If you find yourself in a place where you cannot grasp that connection as hard you try, by all means, get out of there and try somewhere new. You have to take care of yourself and if that means heading up the east coast or heading out west then go for it. I am not saying run away from what you are feeling; face it head-on and accept the responsibility of taking action for what is best for you.

Remember, there are various mental health websites and clinics throughout the country if you ever need professional help.

Everyone at work was complaining of the next Sydney winter. I thought to myself, "I just had the worst winter of my life, there's no way in hell that I am doing that again." So, I looked for jobs in the sun and headed north.

These are some ideas for when you start to feel a loss of connection.

- Look up random free events and schedule yourself to go to one. Get yourself involved with something that you are interested in or something that you want to learn more about. It could be a museum guest speaker, a concert, a local festival of some sort of a surf club gathering. Type in "free events in _____ today" and see what pops up. Whatever appeals to you, get yourself up and do it. You will be happy you did.

- Send postcards to friends and family back home. It doesn't have to say much or really anything at all, but it makes you feel more connected to them being so far away. I am sure they would be very happy to receive one. Stamps are sold in almost every convenience store. "MoonPig" is a great website you can use to send customised cards and you can schedule them in advance to be sent on future dates.

- Remember why you flew across the world. Remember why you are doing what you're doing. Cruising around thinking, "What the f*ck am I doing?" is normal. But, when you start to think about why you want to be in Oz, it brings you a sense of purpose.

- Take a deep breath and think of all the things you are grateful for, especially all the things in Australia you are grateful for. If living and travelling here really isn't for you, then you know you are just a plane ticket away from home.   Give yourself a break and watch how your adventure will unfold.

Resources

Mental Health Help	https://headtohealth.gov.au
Head Space Centres	https://headspace.org.au/our-services/our-centres/
Moon Pig Customised Cards	https://www.moonpig.com/au/

Thought #4: I don't know where I am going to live.

If you have a desire to give the nod to go down the slide at a waterpark, then Sydney or Surfer's Paradise is where you are going to need to reside.

The decision on where you are going to live is up to you, your willingness to job hunt, and what you want to experience during your time in Australia. Australia is massive and it may feel overwhelming looking at a map because there are so many places to choose from. You may be thinking everywhere you go has a kangaroo or everywhere is hot and red dirt, but a little research goes a long way…

Australia is made up of six states and two territories. They are listed below with their corresponding abbreviation and major towns, cities, or areas.

Western Australia (WA)	Perth	Margaret River	Esperance	Broome
Queensland (QLD)	Brisbane	Gold Coast	Sunshine Coast	Cairns
South Australia (SA)	Adelaide	Kangaroo Island	Mt. Gambier	
Tasmania (TAS)	Hobart	Wine Glass Bay	Launceston	
Victoria (VIC)	Melbourne	Torquay	Yarra Valley	
NewSouth Wales (NSW)	Sydney	Wollongong	Lord Howe Island	Byron Bay
Northern Territory (NT)	Alice Springs	Darwin	Katherine	
Australian Capital Territory (ACT)	Canberra			

Australia is located in the southern hemisphere, so the farther south you go, the cooler it will be... The farther north you go, the warmer it will be. You may be tricked to believe that Australia is hot all over, but it does get quite cold in many places; you will need to have a jumper.

Fall	Winter
March, April, May	*June, July, August*
Spring	**Summer**
September, October, November	*December, January, February*

Just like anywhere else in the world, major cities, (Melbourne, Sydney, Adelaide, Perth, and Brisbane) are where the most jobs will be found. However, if you do not want to live in a city, then by all means... don't! So, just give it a try somewhere else if the natural extra expenses that come with living in a city and the whole city life isn't for you! Australia is your playground. When you truly put your mental and physical efforts into finding a job, no matter what it may be, you will find a way to make that happen.

Flatmates is a great website with a free app to use for finding a house or flat to live in Australia. It is the quickest way into finding a place to live; I found my flat within a matter of hours. A great feature of Flatmates is that copious amounts of places listed have flexible renting commitments. If you want to work in Perth for six months but also want to work in the Gold Coast for six months, Flatmates makes it simpler for finding the right home to suit your needs. Even if you want to spend a couple of weeks in Noosa, I am sure with the search filters they offer, you could find a place for that amount of time.

You may be asked to do an "inspection" when inquiring about a place to live. This simply means for the roommates or landlord to meet you and see if you are a good fit as well as for you to see if you think you would like to live there.

It is important to note that rent is usually paid weekly in Australia.

If you are feeling any kind of uneasiness or confusion about where to live, change your thought to how exciting it is to arrive somewhere that you have no idea about! Think to yourself... "Look out Australia, (insert your name here) is about to arrive!"

Questions to ask yourself to help you gain insight and narrow down places on where you may like to live:

- **Does being close to the ocean matter to me?**
- **Do I want to be close to mountains?**
- **What kind of job would I like to have?**
- **Do I want to have my own car?**
- **Do I want to be in a busy or laid-back atmosphere?**
- **Do I need to be close to public transportation?**
- **What do I like to spend my money on?**

If you truly do not know or have at least an idea as to where you would like to be in Australia, it never hurts to throw a dart at a map, see where it lands and head there.

Or, I can be your personal Australian matchmaker, location wise that is.

State Descriptions

These are *very brief* descriptions to give you an idea of what <u>some</u> of the areas of Australia are like in each state.

As you can see from this map, Australia is f*cking huge! I cannot explain to you every single place. However, I can give you some brief details to help guide you further.

My goal is to build you a foundation of geographical knowledge that will aid in your decision on where you would like to live. Think of this as a starting point.

Most of Australia's roughly 25 million population lives on the coast. When you venture far out from cities or highly populated towns, the more rural and remote it becomes in every state and territory.

The Best Roads are Ocean Roads

The beginning of the Great Ocean Road begins in Torquay, Victoria, about an hour and a half southwest of Melbourne.

A highly recommended book to read before going to the Great Ocean Road is 'A Rip Curl Story.' You will learn not only about the iconic brand but also about the history of the area as well.

Melbourne: hip and trendy. It is rich with live music and bustling with art everywhere you look. Its weather is very unpredictable; it could be hot one day and freezing the next. The city is famous for it. It is renowned for its cafe culture, especially vegan cafes, and it's no "lock outlaws" - you can go clubbing all night and then eat breakfast in the club.

Two Words: Hot and Remote

Welcome to the outback! Not much entirely going on except for flies, mining, cattle and dirt, lots and lots of dirt. Everything about the Northern Territory is remote. There are not that many places to reside unless you are in the cattle industry.

Alice Springs is an oasis in the desert of fewer than 30,000 people. It is considered a "linking town" to Uluru (Ayer's Rock). You can learn heaps about the indigenous culture in Australia here, including their beautiful artwork. People are attracted to Darwin for its tropical - cosmopolitan atmosphere, barramundi fishing and how close it is to Asia. There can be very cheap flights to Bali from Darwin.

World-Class Beaches

New South Wales does not disappoint with its remarkable coast. As you travel north or south of Sydney, the more laid back the towns become. Ocean pools are in almost every coastal town.

Sydney has to be one of the most exquisite cities in the world because of how pristine its coastline is. There are other cities in the world that are next to the ocean, but they don't compare with Sydney's natural surrounding beauty.

Sydneyis not as "artsy" as Melbourne, but it is very cosmopolitan; and you can find some of the nicest bars and restaurants here. All you need to do is type "Merivale" into Google. You will not be disappointed going to any that are listed.

Windy West Coast

"WA" has an untouched charm. The beaches are pristine, the water is crystal clear, and is a home to the Ningaloo Reef (Exmouth is the major gateway). A car is a must in West Australia; it is much more dispersed and less populated than the East Coast.

Broome is hot, small, has camels and the main beach is a nudist beach.

Perth has many similarities with Brisbane: smaller than Sydney and Melbourne and has a river, not directly on the ocean. As a city, Perth has a laid-back - suburban feel to it.

South Is Fine, Fine With More Wine

South Australia is known for its vineyards. The Barossa Valley and Adelaide Hills produce some of the world's finest wines. Try the Rockford Shiraz Cab or the Mother Hen Chardonnay.

Wine…
Wine…
And more Wine……………
If you want to work in the wine industry, head south.

The Capital of Australia is… (not Sydney)

Canberra is the capital of Australia. It is west of Sydney within New South Wales, but its own entity; "Australian Capital Territory". There are ski resorts you can reach from Canberra within a few hours' drive as well as wineries, waterfalls and copious amounts of hikes. Canberra has been noted as the "youngest city" in Australia. It is also where you can see an actual kangaroo in an actual city.

Sunny Queensland

Think of Queensland as three different sections of the coast.

South Queensland: Brisbane is in between the Gold Coast and the Sunshine Coast. If you had to compare these coasts in one worded answers: Goldy is party, Sunny is tranquil.

Brisbane is an up and coming city with an increasing amount of nightlife. It is not directly on the ocean, but Morton Bay and Stradbroke Island ("Straddy") are the main attractions close by. You get the "best of both worlds" with Brisbane. A warm weathered city very close to copious amounts of beach towns that are quite easy to get to.

Look for the "Jimmys at Wrightsville Beach" sticker on the way to Tea Tree Bay in Noosa. (@jimmyswrightsvillebeach)

Central Coast Queensland: Between Noosa and Cairns, there are heaps of sub-tropical towns that can lead as "gateways" to the Great Barrier Reef. The population is much more dispersed. From around Gladstone and up, crocodiles begin to make themselves known: "croc city". Agnes Water is the last place with waves in

Queensland; as you go farther north, the coast is protected by the reef, so no waves.

The IPhone's "Siri" is from Mackay!

Far North Queensland: Cairns (pronounced like "cans") is the epicentre of Far North Queensland. It is the most highly regarded place for reaching the Great Barrier Reef. It is a heavy backpacker town; the city thrives off of tourists because of all the attractions that are close by. Cairns CBD is very small; it is perfect for walking everywhere. However, to explore anywhere outside of the CBD, a car is a must, due to the not so reliable bus service.

Wake up Australia, Tasmania is floating away!

Tasmania is the first place for the Antarctic winds to hit; it does get very cold! There are tons of trails and beaches to explore. Hiking, surf, fishing, lakes, camping… Tassy really has it all.

Hobart is a cosy waterfront town filled with the finest fresh oysters, lobster and abalone. Everything is within walking distance, however, if you really want to explore Tasmania, a car is vital; the bus only goes so far.

Something fun to do in Tassy: while driving for stretches at a time, whatever winery you see, stop there and go to the free wine tasting. Just make sure you have a designated driver…

Airport Help

Australian Border Patrol is very strict. Even if you don't think you need to declare it...declare it!

Melbourne

- Skybus will take you into the Central Business District (CBD). Skybusses will be found at most airports throughout Australia.
- You can buy a ticket online in advance or just go right up to the kiosk and purchase there. It is $19.75 AUD one-way.
- Where they drop you off in the CBD is where you will go to return to the airport with Skybus.
- If bringing your cat or dog to Australia is a deal breaker for you, then Melbourne is the only airport that you are eligible to fly into; mandatory ten day quarantine is based outside of this airport.

Sydney

- The train to the CBD of Sydney is in the airport - it is very convenient. It is about $17 AUD one-way to Circular Quay. Make sure you read the signs and are on the right side of the tracks when boarding the train.
- You will need the NSW Opal Card. The kiosk is on the left before you swipe through to go to the train.

Brisbane

- The "Airtrain" at the Brisbane Airport runs north into the Sunshine Coast, to Brisbane Central, and down south into the Gold Coast.

- You can purchase tickets online or use a GoCard. The ticket prices vary, depending on how north or how south you travel.
- It is $19.50 AUD one-way to get from the airport to Brisbane Central.

Cairns

- Cairns is much smaller than the other major arriving cities. The best option is to take an Uber or taxi to where you are staying in Cairns. The bus is very unreliable.
- Shopping, restaurant, and pub wise, everything is within walking distance in Cairns.
- If you plan on staying for a longer period of time in Cairns, a car would be a must; there is much to explore on the outskirts and beyond the CBD.

Perth

- If you land in terminals 3 or 4, you can board the public bus route 40 that will take you to Elizabeth Quay Bus Station, which is in the Perth CBD.
- If you land in terminals 1 or 2, you can board the public bus route 380 to Elizabeth Quay Bus Station. You can buy your tickets at Transperth Booths at the airport.
- Tickets are under $5 AUD one-way.

Adelaide

- The airport has a bus service called JetExpress that can take you into the city. The bus leaves every thirty minutes and has many stops.

Hobart

- The SkyBus will take you directly into Hobart. There are different stops made along the way. If you are confused about which stop to get off at, just let the bus driver know where you are staying and he or she will tell you where to get off.

- You can buy the ticket as you board the bus. The SkyBus ticket is $19.50 AUD one-way.

Gold Coast/Ballina

- If your plan is to go to Byron Bay from either the Gold Coast or Ballina airports, The Byron Bay Shuttle is the cheapest option.
- It is $30 one-way from Ballina and $32 one-way from Gold Coast. They will pick you up from the airport and drop you off exactly where you are staying.

Resources

Flat mates	https://flatmates.com.au
Sydney Airport Transport	https://www.sydneyairport.com.au/info-sheet/transport-options-domestic
Melbourne Airport Transport	https://www.melbourneairport.com.au/Passengers/To-from-the-airport/Buses-shuttles
Perth Airport Transport	https://www.perthairport.com.au/to-and-from-the-airport/transport-options/public-transport.
Adelaide Airport Transport	https://www.adelaideairport.com.au/parking-transport/transport-options/public-transport/

Cairns Airport Transport	https://www.cairnsairport.com.au/travelling/parking-and-transport/transport-options/
Brisbane Airport Transport	https://www.bne.com.au/passenger/to-and-from/transport-options
Byron Bay Shuttle	https://www.byronbayshuttle.com.au
Bringing your cat or dog to Australia via Melbourne	https://www.agriculture.gov.au/cats-dogs

Thought #5: How do I set up a bank account? How do I get a phone number?

Pay attention. You can wing it more in the fun stuff once you tackle the "technical" stuff.

There are three different banks in Australia to choose from. ANZ, Commonwealth, or Westpac. As a foreigner, you can't really go wrong with any of them. I chose Westpac because it was the closest one to walk to and there wasn't a line—I really didn't feel like standing in a line that day.

You can sign up for your bank account online, up to three months before coming to Australia. However, to withdraw money, you will need to go into the Australian bank in person to verify you are you. Don't forget to let your home bank know that you are heading to Australia before you get here.

The only currency accepted in Australia is Australian Dollars (AUD). Go to your home bank and have some exchanged for you or just wait until you get to Australia. My suggestion, though, is to go ahead and exchange some cash before you leave, it will be helpful when you get off the plane.

Just like anywhere, you can use your home bank card to dispense cash from Australian ATMs, but remember there is a transaction fee that you cannot get around.

Something great about Australia's currency and price system is that goods and services tax (GST), is included in 99.99% of all prices. If a product says it's $5, it is. You pay that at the checkout line and nothing more.

There are ways with each of these banks for you to be able to transfer from your home account into your new Australian account. However, it is so much easier and there are less fees to use TransferWise. TransferWise is an app that moves money from and into foreign accounts. The fee tends to be no more than $5 AUD, it is completely safe, and your money will enter the chosen account within a couple of days. If you decide to set up your bank account before coming to Australia, go ahead and do this. When you enter the bank to verify your identity and receive your new debit card, you will already have money ready to go.

If you are used to using the app "Venmo," it does not exist (yet) in Australia. You can still use it with your home country bank account, but Australian bank accounts are not available to use through it. Instead, Australian banks make it easy for you to pay through your actual bank account to any other Australian bank account. For instance, say someone buys your lunch and you want to pay them back. You can go into your Australian bank account under the "Pay" tab, enter their full name, their BSB number, account number and the amount you want to pay them.

The two main phone carriers of Oz are Telstra and Optus.

When you get off the plane, you can go to any Coles, Woolies, or convenience store inside the airport to purchase a prepaid phone number card. There are all different options regarding the amount of data and time usage provided. You will receive a new SIM card with this prepaid card—make sure you keep your "home SIM card" in a safe place.

Once you have your prepaid card, go somewhere with Wi-Fi - Australia is great with public Wi-Fi - download the Telstra or Optus app. Follow the instructions and select your plan.

When you get to the part where they ask you for an address to determine what geographical phone number they will give you, well, since you are brand new to Australia, you do not have an address yet. So, just type in a public place in any town. For example, type in "Comedy Club" in Sydney and you will see a bunch of different numbers pop up. Select one from the given list and that is your new Aussie number. They don't keep this address on file, they just need a place to work with to decide a number for you.

Phone numbers in Australia are pronounced:

123-334-556 - "One, two, triple three, four, double five, six"

Double and triple are used to describe any number or letter in a row.

It is important to note that for a vast number of areas in Australia, phone service either does not exist or only one phone company, generally Telstra, is offered. If you are led to going to a remote place, research this subject before you go. However, if you are in highly populated areas, no worries.

Before leaving, don't forget to let your home phone company know that you are going to Australia for an extended amount of time. They can help you set up a cheaper or suspended plan account since you will not be using it in Australia.

There once was a time where two were given the responsibility of taking care of an island. A beautiful day, like always, crystal blue water and the sun shining bright. When an unexpected noise came from the sky, a moment of slight panic arose. Is it the feds?! Is it an intruder?! The chopper landed on the glistening sand. "Welcome to the Island, how can I help you??" is all that can be said.

"We're Telstra. We're here to fix your phones."

Telstra. Telstra always pulls through.

You cannot work in Australia without setting up your tax file number, "TFN." It is linked to your Superannuation fund, commonly referred to as your "Super." The Superannuation fund is just like a retirement account. When you begin to work, part of your paycheck is deposited into this account by your employer. To set up a Super account, you must have your TFN first. You can do both of these tasks online.

When you leave Australia, and you don't plan on coming back to work, you can access your Super account and withdraw from it. There are certain steps you will need to take to do this, but I advise you to not think too much about this process at the beginning of your move. I have provided the link for you for informational purposes, but it is not a top priority until you decide when you will return to your home place.

Resources

Anz Bank Account	https://www.anz.com.au/personal/bank-accounts/moving-to-australia/en/
Commonwealth Bank Account	https://www.commbank.com.au/moving-to-australia/banking.html
Westpac Bank Account	https://www.westpac.com.au/personal-banking/bank-accounts/transaction/choice/migrants/
Set up a Tax File Number	https://iar.ato.gov.au/IARWeb/default.aspx?pid=4&sid=1&outcome=1
Set up a Superannuation Account	https://www.sunsuper.com.au/memberjoinonline#step-0
Superannuation Details	https://www.ato.gov.au/individuals/super/
Claimingyour Superannuation when leaving Australia	https://immi.homeaffairs.gov.au/entering-and-leaving-australia/leaving-australia
Telstra	https://www.telstra.com.au.
Optus	https://www.optus.com.au/mobile

Thought #6: How am I going to find a job?

I highly recommend taking UberPool rides and chatting up whoever you are sharing the ride with. Ya never know, they could end up offering you a job.
When searching and applying for jobs, engrave these two words into your mind:

Conversation
&
Persistence

When you are sitting at the bus stop, talk to the person next to you. When you are in an UberPool, talk to the people in your Uber. When you are sitting in a cafe, talk to people around you. Even if you are not a big talker, build a bridge and get over it, and talk to people. And trust me, if you are not keen on talking to people, you will definitely be by the first week if you are by yourself here.

You never know who you are going to meet or talk to that could lead to a job, so just start talking.

When you are applying for a job in Australia, persistence is going to be what separates you from the rest. There are tons and tons of people on working holiday visas searching for jobs. I will tell you, it is not easy. But, persistence is what will get you the job. Keep emailing, keep calling, keep texting the business, the owner, the hiring manager, etc.… **Basically, be really annoying.**

You need to be positive and ruthless.

Persistence shows that you care and that you want to work, not just fill up space. If you show with your heart and soul that you want to work and that you bring great skills to the table, then an employer is going to choose you over someone that doesn't demonstrate that 99.99% of the time. You cannot get discouraged if you don't hear back from employers or get no's. This is where persistence comes into play as well. You have to get back up and keep trying. It can be a tough job market when you are an expat, but do not let that deter you. When you really put yourself out there and apply with confidence, you will achieve acquiring a job in Australia.

The two main websites to search for jobs in Oz are: Gumtree and Seek. If you are still in your home country, you can take a look at the websites to just get an idea of what they are and the kinds of jobs that are out there. Employers would rather you be in the country whilst applying; you are much more reliable that way.

Australia's hospitality and tourism industry accounts for a huge part of the country's economy; this is where a majority of jobs are. However, follow your interests and expand on your skills to see where it takes you.

Go on Instagram and type in, for a place or tag such as: "Esperance." Take a look at what businesses pop up. See one that interests you? Dive deep into their DMs and message them asking if they are hiring as well as give them a few nice details about yourself and let them know that you have a work visa. Then dive deep into their website, phone number, email….

Congratulations.

You are now an Australian Job Detective.

Also, don't limit yourself to just these two job websites. LinkedIn and Facebook are great too. Do some investigating and search your little heart out. Whether that is walking around looking at businesses or flyers posted on public bulletin boards.

Don't forget: conversation.

You will have a greater advantage when applying for hospitality jobs if you already have an "RSA." An RSA stands for *Responsible Service of Alcohol*. It is a requirement to have this certificate while working at an establishment that serves alcohol. Each state has certain requirements regarding the RSA; an RSA acquired in one state can be used in a different state, but for some, you have to get a new certificate if moving to a different state.

All states, except NSW and VIC, allows you to use an RSA interchangeably; you don't have to redo the course if you move from WA to TAS. But, you do if you move to NSW or VIC from any other state.

You can take the course online and the cost varies per state. Victoria is the only state that requires you to sign up for a virtual classroom; for all the other states, you can take it at your own speed and time. The cost of this course varies between $20 and $100.

The course is basically to understand the regulations of serving drinks, kicking drunk people out of the bar and what happens if you break the rules. There is a portion at the end where you have to speak and write. Make sure you take those parts somewhat seriously or else you will have to redo them; it is graded.

A few drinks you should know how to make:

Aperol Spritz

Lemon, Lime & Bitters

Espresso Martini

There are two other certificates that are an advantage depending on what industry you will work in: "RSG" (Responsible Service of Gambling) and a "White Card." RSG is required for working in a venue with gambling and a white card is required for working in construction.

You have to be in Australia to take these courses.
Before taking each course, you will be prompted to create a "Unique Student Identifier," (USI) number. This is just simply a "vault" of all certifications you acquire while in Australia. You also have to be in Australia to create this account. When filling out your details, make sure you fill out the information the exact way it appears on your passport.

Restaurants and bars will have you perform a "trial shift." On your first day, the manager wants to see how well you work. You don't get much training at all; you are thrown straight into it. Look over the establishment's menu the night before, to get a glimpse of what you will be serving. You will have a greater advantage if you prepare.

If you have never waited tables before, these tips may guide you in a successful direction:

1. *Look in the mirror, smile and say: "Yo, Yo, Yo!" (It builds confidence and character).*

2. *Repeat the words "Five Stars" in your head as you enter the restaurant. You are a five star person.*

3. *Think about all the times you go out to eat and what you like about your waiter and what you don't like, be like the good one.*

4. *Double check that you write everything down correctly.*

5. *Remember, all people want to do when they go out to a restaurant is eat what they order, drink what they order, have a good time, and smile. Make that happen.*

A resume in Australia is referred to as a curriculum vitae, "CV." A CV is longer and lists out all of your specific accomplishments. Basically, just think of a CV as an in depth resume. Even though that is a brief definition, when writing your CV for jobs in Oz, just write a normal resume like you would anywhere else. CV is just what it is referred to in Australia.

CV Template

<table>
<tr><td>Your
Picture here</td><td>Name
Australian Phone Number
Email
Home Country
Type of Visa</td></tr>
</table>

1. State what certifications you hold and that you are willing to acquire more that could be beneficial to the job position.

2. State the specific skills you have that directly relate to the position you are applying for.

3. Give a detailed description of why, with your experience, hard work, positivity and skills, you are the best fit for the position. You are selling yourself as the solution to their problem.

Work Experience: List up to three jobs that have relevance to the position you are applying for. You may have to give a brief description of who or what you worked for because the employer may have no idea what it is. List up to three valuable duties or achievements that add credit to you being the best candidate for the open position.

Education: State the highest form of education you have as well as any degrees that are directly geared toward the position you are applying for. Keep it short and simple.

"Thank you for you taking the time to read my CV. I look forward to hearing from you." - Your Name.

Applying to Jobs Checklist

- Bank Account Details
  - Your Name
  - Bank Name
  - BSB Number
  - Account Number

- Tax File Number

- A copy of your granted work holiday visa

- A copy of your granted RSA, RSG, or White Card certificates (if working in hospitality or construction)

- Your Passport

- Your *perfected* CV printed out or in PDF for online applications

Persistence
Positivity
Ruthlessness

Resources

Gumtree	https://www.gumtree.com.au.
Seek	https://www.seek.com.au.
RSA Queensland	https://www.eot.edu.au/online-courses/RSA/QLD/
RSA Victoria	https://www.eot.edu.au/online-courses/RSA/VIC/
RSA West Australia	https://www.eot.edu.au/online-courses/RSA/WA/
RSA New South Wales	https://www.eot.edu.au/online-courses/RSA/NSW/
RSA Tasmania	https://www.eot.edu.au/online-courses/RSA/TAS/
RSA South Australia	https://www.eot.edu.au/online-courses/RSA/SA/
RSA Northern Territory	https://www.eot.edu.au/online-courses/RSA/NT/
RSA Australian Capital Territory	https://www.eot.edu.au/online-courses/RSA/ACT/

RCG/RSG	https://www.eot.edu.au/online-courses/RSG/
White Card	https://www.eot.edu.au/online-courses/white-card/
USI	https://www.usi.gov.au

Thought #7: I want to travel, but I don't want to blow through all of my money.

Time really is of the essence... Especially if you are thinking you will be one of those people who underestimate how massive Australia is. You cannot effectively try to travel from Sydney to Cairns in less than a week and say that you have "seen" Australia.

Life is not Instagram.

Don't just travel to a place because you feel like you have to, just to say you've been there or to get a few likes on social media.
Go where you truly want to go. Do what you want to do. Not from what a guidebook tells you. Not even from me. All the travel guidebooks in the world are meant for informing, detailing and helping. I can talk to you all day about my favourite places in this world and why I think you should go there, but when it comes

down to it, go where you want to go. It's your time. And if you don't know where, that's okay, neither do I, most of the time. Follow what interests you, step out of your comfort zone and go with it.

The four best ways for saving money on accommodation while you are not working in Australia are described below. Each of them have their pros and their cons. But, all of them will help you not splurge on just a night's sleep.

Hostels
It is rare to find a "bad" hostel in Australia. Any town, in higher populated areas, you are bound to find at least one they are great for meeting people, hearing about open jobs, and asking for any advice. The best way to find the cheapest deals and book the fastest way is through the free Hostelworld app.

When you are confronted with hundreds of hostels to choose from, especially when you are in Sydney or Melbourne, these four aspects will help you narrow down your decision:

1. Ratings: read the reviews. If someone takes the time to actually write a review on Hostelworld, they must feel deeply for what they are writing.

2. Price: prices will be higher in cities; it is inevitable.

3. Location: is it within walking distance to the areas you would like to explore? Or close to public transportation?

4. Kitchen/Free Breakfast: if it does not have either of these two, then you will end up spending even more money on having to eat out for your meals.

With these four factors, you will often have to compromise. It all depends on what is most important to you. I always like to stay as close to the ocean as possible. So, if that means paying an extra $10 a night, I will do it.

If you are on the quest for a good night's sleep every night, then I do not suggest you stay in a party hostel…

helpx.net
Do not be fooled by the outdated 2005 looking website; Helpx is in fact, the real deal. It is a help exchange platform. A "host" will provide you free accommodation and meals in exchange for you helping them with a project for a few hours a day. The projects range from gardening, babysitting, building, cleaning… it all varies. The cost is $22 USD/year. This website is worth the twenty bucks; the amount of money it saves you, even if you only stay with the host for a few days, could be in the hundreds.

I did it. And if I hadn't done it, I would have never met Hippy Jim.

Hippy Jim resided in Mission Beach where the cassowaries roamed free. An original American Southern man dreamed of Australia with his newlywed Aussie wife. A diner on the city outskirts is what he created and adored. But, twenty years later, a slip on cucumber in the junction left him with quite a few broken limbs. The jungle was calling his name. He packed up his things and made a life in the bush where the cassowaries roam free.

workaway.info
Workaway is another work exchange site, with the same concept of Helpx. It is $44 USD/year. If you are with a friend or partner, you can sign up together and the cost is cheaper. I have found that it is harder to receive replies from hosts on Workaway than it is on Helpx.

Is there a surf break that you really want to go to, but want to minimise your costs while you are there? Type into the search bar "Margaret River Surf" and see what pops up. There could be a host that needs help with cleaning around the house that could live right on the beach or offer to take you to the best spots.

Whatever hobby or skill you have and whatever place you want to go to, type it into the search bar and see where it takes you. The opportunities are endless. You could learn something new, you make a new friend, and of course, you will save money. It can be quite rewarding too.

couchsurfing.com
Couchsurfing is set up just like the two previously mentioned websites, but there is rarely any "work" involved. It is a free website. I typically see Couchsurfing as a last resort. It is nice if

you really just need a place to crash for a night or two and also to have a super local experience.

Helpx, Workaway, and Couchsurfing all have review options for each host. Make sure you read them and see if it is for you. Especially in Australia, it's hard to meet an unkind person, but just remember, reading the reviews of your host is important.

Camping
If you have a car, camping is the way to go. Even if you don't find yourself much as a "camper," camping in Australia has to be one of the easiest and most serene places to do it. When you are in popular areas, make sure you read up on rules and regulations; there are heaps of camping sites/caravan parks. If you are pretty rural, it's pretty much just finding where you are going to want to park yourself for the night, however, beware of the parking rangers.

There are four major grocery stores throughout Australia:

Aldi $
Coles $$
IGA $$$
Woolworths (Woolies) $$$

Going to a local farmers' market, usually on Sundays, will always be a cheaper option than the four major stores.

When travelling for long stretches of time, simply purchasing a loaf of bread, a jar of peanut butter, a jar of jam, a bag of apples, and a pack of Tim Tams, will help you not spend so much on the overpriced snacks. Don't forget a knife!

Due to the "tap" on debit and credit cards when making a purchase and now the option to have your phone tap to pay, you lose a sense of what you are doing. Taking out a set amount of cash that you want to spend for the week helps you manage where your money is going as well as actually paying attention to what you are doing, instead of mindlessly tapping your card.

It is wise to just spend your money on food at the grocery stores. Toilet paper, shampoo, camping necessities, etc. can all be purchased for cheaper at stores like:

The Reject Shop
Dinki D Discounts
Chemist Warehouse
Vinnies
Red Cross
Salvation Army

Airtasker is a website where people post a "task" that they will pay you to help them with. Tasks vary from helping to move a refrigerator to creating a website. You "bid" on the task and explain why you are the best for the job. This could be a great way to make a few extra bucks whilst traveling.

You can read about cheaper transportation options for traveling throughout Australia in thought #9.

Resources

Hostelworld	https://www.hostelworld.com
Helpx	https://www.helpx.net.
Workaway	https://www.workaway.info.
CouchSurfing	https://www.couchsurfing.com
AirTasker	https://www.airtasker.com

Thought #8: Doesn't everything in Australia kill you?

Apparently, a lot of people in the world believe that all the animals in Australia can kill you. Yes, some can. But, the chances of that happening are slim. So, chill out.

Cassowaries

The dinosaur bird. Looks like an ostrich. Kind of creepy. But has the potential to be cute in a certain type of way. Mostly found around Mission Beach, you do not want to get snuck up behind this bird. Their feet could be twice the size of your head, they cannot fly but they can run. They are super keen on fruit; do not carry fruit in your bag if you are going on a hike in the bush. Go on YouTube and look up a video of one.

Crocodiles

The modern day dinosaur... Northwest Australia, Northern Territory and North Queensland make up what I like to call: *"croc city."* God forbid you ever come into close contact with a crocodile, but if you do, remember these words:

1. You can outrun a crocodile if you are on hard sand; now, if you are on thick sinking sand that may be a little more difficult. They can start out running fast as they dart or jump out, but they cannot sustain stamina. They do not like to waste their energy.

2. Strive to jab the eyes and ears if attacked. If a crocodile loses the capability to see or hear, it will not be able to survive due to how vital these senses are to hunting. Crocs are extremely sensitive. Any kind of pain or the threat of pain will scare them away. That shows a misconception about crocs - they are actually quite cowardly.

3. If you see a dark stick floating in the water in croc city, keep your eye on it, if it ends up moving, it could quite possibly be one.

4. Crocs like murky water, especially in areas with mangroves. Crocodiles have to believe that they can drown you to attack. If they do not, then they will not make the move. They are stalkers and hunters. They will watch you and they will understand your patterns to the point where, if you are not wary, they could take you down.

5. Do not swim in croc city areas at night. Maybe that is obvious, but it is amazing what alcohol can do to you.

A croc hunter once told me, "Run like hell, kid."

Mantis Shrimp
Contrary to popular belief, Manties are the fastest animal in the world due to the hunting reflex of their front claw, closing faster than the speed of sound. Since they are such hidden creatures living in sand tunnels below the surface, it can be hard to know the exact places they reside. However, they definitely live in North Queensland. Manties have extremely sharp "teeth" on their front claw as well as on the back of their tails. Sixteen cones in their eyes give them the most complex vision out of any animal on the planet. So intense that they have been used for detecting cancer cells. They can see things that we will never be able to fathom.

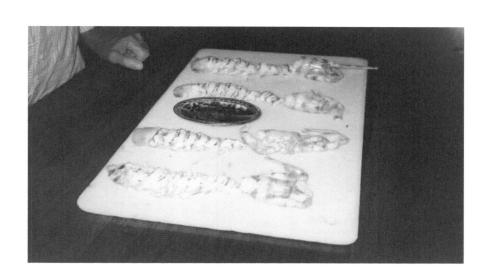

Thought #9: How do I get around the country?

When someone offers you a free ride and you are basically quite broke, you take it. Even if it is in an 18-Wheeler truck.

I come from a place where public transportation is pretty much non-existent. I find Australia's to be easy and simple to figure out.

Each major city, excluding Cairns, has a transportation card you can obtain at the airport or generally at any convenience store.

This card is rechargeable through kiosks dispersed throughout the cities, through the card's app on your phone or inside convenient stores.

You tap the card each time you hop on or hop off public transportation, including the bus, ferry, light rail, tram and train.

Each state has a different card; you cannot use the NSW card while in QLD and vice-versa. When you cross borders, it is wise to acquire a new card for the new state you are in.

Victoria	Myki Pass	South Australia	MetroCard
New South Wales	Opal	Northern Territory	Tap & Ride
Queensland	GoCard	Tasmania	GreenCard
West Australia	SmartRider	Australian Capital Territory	MyWay

Off you hop!

For long distance travel, there are two major bus lines: Premier and Greyhound. Premier is generally cheaper. However, you will have more value for your money with Greyhound. Greyhound includes Wi-Fi, comfy-ish seats, takes less rest stops (trust me, if you are on an overnight bus trip, you do not want to have to stop every two hours) and a selection of travel passes.

The Greyhound travel passes are referred to as "hop on and hop off." It is great if you are travelling along the coast in one direction for a set amount of time. Do not purchase this ticket if you are deciding to travel up and down or back and forth, because you can only go in one direction. I think it is an amazing deal because you can go to so many places on your own time. I find the best hop on and hop off pass is valid for 90 days of travel. There are other passes that give you more freedom instead of just going in one direction, however, they are much dearer. Take a look at the website and see which one is best for you.

The train is quite a journey. There are a few routes that are specialised in the scenic route: taking the train for the pure fun of it. However, if striving to save a couple extra hundred bucks and see the country side of Australia, then "all aboard choo choo," this is a great option. The train does make many stops, but only for a very short period of time, so make sure you pay attention when your stop is. Be prepared that your phone may die due to no charging ports; keep a spare copy of where you are headed. It might be useful to have a portable charger on you.

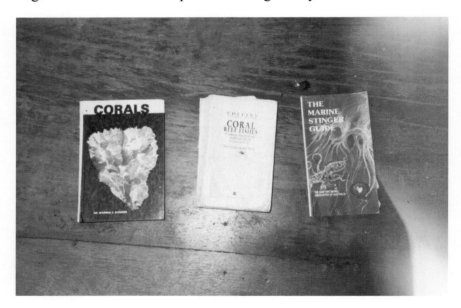

If you are super keen on driving, especially if you are not living in one of the major cities, buying a car when you are in Australia is something to consider heavily. It gives you freedom to go to places on your own time and get to places public transportation cannot take you, which is a majority of the country. It is especially vital for exploring national parks.

Australia drives on the left hand side of the road in kilometres per hour (kph). If you have never driven on the left hand side of the road before, you are going to need to take a big deep breath in and believe that you can do it. Focusing on the lines will help you. Do some practice drives on less populated roads before joining in with the big dogs.

The legal driving alcohol limit of Australia is .05% BAC.

The average cost of a used car is between $5,000 and $15,000 AUD. There are copious second hand dealerships that you can purchase from. People are always selling their cars, especially expats, so finding one is going to be no worries. Carsales, Gumtree, and Facebook are helpful websites to aid in your search.

To be honest, the only land vehicle I have ever driven, so far, in Australia is a BobCat. But, I research and talk to people so the information below can help you.

Each state has their own rules, regulations and processes of buying and selling cars. The information below is generally speaking for Australia. You can research the state you decide to buy from and see the specifics of what is needed and where to go to for any "technical" paperwork sorts of things.

- Registration or "rego" is mandatory when acquiring a car. If you do not have it, you cannot drive (legally). For validity, it must be in the name of the owner of the car, so it is important to transfer the name from whomever you are purchasing from. Rego could already be "valid" when you purchase your car. Meaning that all you need to do is transfer the name, not buy another round of rego. Rego is valid for one year, but can be requested for shorter lengths of time, which would be great for travelling. The price of rego is correlated with the price of your car.

- Obtaining a roadworthy certificate, aka passing inspection, is required when purchasing a car. It is commonly referred to as a "pink slip." Just like with rego, you cannot drive without this certificate.
- A certain level of insurance is included in your rego, it will cover any kind of costs relating to your injury if you were to be in an accident. Any other kind of car insurance is not required in Australia, but it is very wise to purchase it. What if you accidentally hit a wallaby? And your car is now totaled? And you now have to sit on the side of the road trying to mend the wallaby and your car? Get the extra insurance.

- You can drive in Australia with your home country license or what is called an "overseas license" for the duration of your stay. You do not need to get a new license unless you are becoming a permanent resident. (On a working holiday visa you are classified as a temporary resident). Make sure it will not expire while you are in Australia. If it does, make an appointment to renew it before you leave, just in case. If your license is not in English, you will need to provide a translated license.

Parking lots are called "car parks" in Australia.

Road tripping for a certain amount of time? Renting a camper van is an option, especially if you share the expenses with other people. There are camp grounds all over Australia and when you are in a more remote place, sides of the road should be fine. When camping, remember to read signs carefully in what you can and cannot do. Especially if you are in a highly populated area. It is easy to get a fine if you are not paying attention.

If you are planning on embarking on a journey through the Outback, it is not as "simple" as a journey from Sydney to Cairns. It is entirely different terrain, temperatures, and remoteness hard to compare with other places in the world. You could have instances where you do not see a petrol station for days or maybe more importantly, water. You must prepare, or it could really be life or death.

There are multiple ride share groups on Facebook where people are constantly posting that they have empty seats to fill and would like some company. Usually, all people ask is to chip in with petrol. You can also ask if anyone has room for you to ride with them. Odds are, you will get tons of responses. It can be quite a commitment to ride with a stranger for eight hours in a car. It is a wonderful way to get to know someone, but remember that you will be inside a car with them for a while. I recommend meeting up with the person before leaving to see if you are going to feel comfortable riding in a car with them for a stretch of time.

I took a free ride with a man for a day and a half. The conversation was okay for the first half of the trip. But then, it slowly faded into only being asked if I have been to Las Vegas on the hour, every hour. My answer was: "No, but I am sure it is fun". Every single time. After a dodgy rest stop and getting dropped off on the side of the road, I thankfully made it back to Noosa.

Plane tickets are not so cheap in Australia, even just from Cairns to Brisbane. But, flying can be the fastest and cheapest form of transportation depending on how far you are travelling.

Qantas and JetStar are the two main airlines of Australia. Qantas is the reigning champion, but Jetstar is great for cheaper tickets, as long as you really don't mind the frequently unexpected cancellations or delays.

Fly across the world for a wedding and the person who invited you to be their "plus one's" JetStar flight gets cancelled and can't attend the wedding... Oh the irony...

It is important to remember that with JetStar, if your carryon bags exceed 7 kilos (15.4 pounds), you will have to pay sixty bucks to get on the flight. To save you this expense, if you think that your bags are going to weigh more than that and you are not that great at sneakily taking those heavy shoes out of your bag until you board the plane, pay at the check in counter. You will still have to pay but it will be a lot cheaper than sixty dollars.

There are tour companies that can help you with your travel plans and that are extremely informative. PeterPan is great for booking discounted bus passes. However, if you ever see a tour company establishment, it is best to cross the street as quickly as possible or else you will be hounded with questions by the staff. No hard feelings on the people working, I know they are just doing their job, but cross the street.

Resources

Greyhound	https://www.greyhound.com.au
Premier	https://www.premierms.com.au
Driving with an Overseas License	https://info.australia.gov.au/information-and-services/transport-and-regional/driving-with-an-overseas-licence
Rego	https://info.australia.gov.au/information-and-services/transport-and-regional/registration-renewal
Pink Slip - SA	https://www.sa.gov.au/topics/driving-and-transport/vehicles/vehicle-inspections/roadworthy-inspections
Pink Slip - NT	https://nt.gov.au/driving/rego/vehicle-inspections/authorised-vehicle-inspectors
Pink Slip - QLD	https://www.qld.gov.au/transport/registration/roadworthy
Pink Slip - NSW	https://www.service.nsw.gov.au/transaction/esafety-checks-pink-slips
Pink Slip - WA	https://www.transport.wa.gov.au/licensing/get-a-vehicle-inspected.asp

Pink Slip - ACT	https://www.accesscanberra.act.gov.au/app/answers/detail/a_id/83/~/motor-vehicle-inspections
Pink Slip - VIC	https://www.vicroads.vic.gov.au/registration/roadworthiness/get-a-certificate-of-roadworthiness
Car Insurance	https://insurance.woolworths.com.au/car-insurance.html
Car Sales	https://www.carsales.com.au
Trains	https://railmaps.com.au
JetStar	https://www.jetstar.com/au/en/home?adults=1&children=0&flexible=1&flight-=&flight-type=2&infants=0&origin=SYD&tab=1
Hopper	https://www.hopper.com
Peter Pan Tour Group	https://peterpans.com/australia/
Greyhound	https://www.greyhound.com.au

Premier	https://www.premierms.com.au

Thought #10: I want to stay in Australia, but I don't know how.

To tell you the truth: once you go to Australia, you are not going to want to leave. Luckily, there are ways to stay longer than what the first year working holiday visa allows. Or you could always marry an Aussie.

Second and third year working holiday visas are available. Unlike the first year, you must complete extra requirements in order to apply.

The Australian government likes to use working holiday visa holders to help the rural and remote areas due to the hard issue of not being able to fill in these jobs with Aussies. In fact, the country heavily relies on expats to work in the agricultural and tourism industries. Without expats to do this work, part of Australia's economy is negatively affected.

Australia wants you here...

To be eligible for a second year working holiday visa, you must work for at least 88 days of a government-approved job in a qualified zip code. These 88 days are commonly referred to as: farm work.

Types of farm work include, but are not limited to fruit picking, construction, mining, bushfire recovery, tree farming, plant and animal work. There is an entire eligibility list of what will count and will not. It would suck if you did something that didn't count, so make sure you triple check it is an eligible job! The 417 and 462 visas have the same requirements, however, only 462 visa holders can work in tourism or hospitality in remote Australia to count for their 88 days.

I am sure you are now asking: "But, how do I find this work? How do I do it?" This is where you put everything you have learned from this book into use. Persistence and Conversation. Asking people within your vicinity, searching on job boards, asking the people at work, asking the people that work at your hostel... It comes with persistence and talking to people.

You will do whatever it takes if you really want to stay in Australia.

Deciding whether or not you want to put the effort into finding regional work is important. You need to think about whether you really want to spend your energy on finding the work or simply enjoy your year in Australia without it. You also need to take into consideration that the working and living conditions, especially for fruit picking, can be quite rigorous. You need to make sure you are receiving payment and that the employer is not dodgy nor keeping you locked in a cellar somewhere in the Outback. I am kidding. (Sort of.)

I know the words "fruit picking" do not sound extremely glamorous... but it could lead you to more opportunities in

Australia. You could learn a bunch of new skills and meet new people that could connect you with other jobs or places to go to. A perk of working in rural and remote areas is that there are not many things to spend your money on. You have a greater ability to save a huge amount of cash. When setting forth in your farm work escapade, go into it with a positive attitude. Your attitude is what will make you or break you.

I had no idea that my job in tourism and hospitality in remote Australia would be eligible towards farm work when I started working. I didn't even know 2nd year visas were an option.

When applying for your second year working holiday visa, unlike the first time you apply, you can apply for it while still in the country. But, you must be in the country when it is granted. *Wait to hop over to Bali until it is granted.* You can also apply for the visa outside of the country, but you have to be outside of Australia for it to be granted.

Once you have the 88 days completed, you can wait to apply for the visa any time before you turn 31 (the exception is Irish, Canadian and French Citizens, it is 35). So, if you wanted to go home for a year or two and then come back, you can. As long as you have all the requirements of the farm work. But, the day your second year visa is granted, you have exactly one year to come back. The same goes for your first year visa. Do not apply for the second year visa if you are out of the country until you know exactly when you would like to go back just in case you miss your "year" mark.

If your application has not been granted yet, and your first visa is about to expire while in Australia, do not fret! You will be placed on what is called a "bridging visa." This is simply just a visa stating you are legally allowed in the country, but you just cannot work yet. It is nothing to stress over. Think of it as a "waiting" visa. It would be very rare for your bridging visa to not be accepted if you have all the correct requirements.

I applied for my second year work holiday visa in the height of a world pandemic, so I guess you could say my situation is a little different than yours. However, I applied for it while in Australia. If the world had not been closed down and I wanted to go to Bali, I would not have been able to. I applied for the visa in Oz, so I would have to stay in Oz until it was granted.

You apply for the second year visa the same way you applied for your first year working holiday visa, through your "immi" account. The same documents that you used for your first application are needed again. The new sets of documents that you must provide are pay stubs from your specified 88 days as well as specific details regarding the work you did.

With a second year working holiday visa, you can work for the same employer you had before for another six months. Remember, you can also go back and forth to Australia as you please while the visa is in use. Go on a trip to Bali, New Zealand or Fiji since you are so close!

Third year working holiday visas are available just like the second year. The same criteria is required, however instead of 88 days of farm work, you have to do 179 days (six months) during your second year stay. You don't have to do six months straight, you can do two, three month stints from eligible jobs and zip codes to qualify for a third year.

There is no fourth year working holiday visas. So, if you deeply want to continue your stay in Oz, you are either going to have to find a partner to get a "partner visa", get sponsored, or you escape into the bush where the government could potentially not track you down.

You will often hear the word "sponsored" in regard to employment. An employer can "sponsor" you because you add value and hold specific skills to the business leading to a longer stay in Australia. Think of sponsorship as the "next level." It is a commitment and a "pass" to living and working in Australia for a greater amount of time. Sponsorship is something that you and your employer would need to talk about if it is something you want to pursue.

If you have a trade, or specific skills, you have a greater chance of qualifying to stay in Australia for much longer. Often referred to as a "tradee". Electrical, construction, mechanical, and plumbing are to name a few. These are sought after skills that are high demand in Australia. If you would like to live in Australia for a long amount of time as an expat, look into acquiring trade - like skills.

As I have stated previously, there is a lot of information regarding visas. But, do not let any of the technical information overwhelm you. It is a lot to take in, but when you log on to the website and start applying, it is actually a lot simpler than you think it may be. If you do get super confused for some reason, I am happy to answer any questions you have.

Resources

Eligible 462 Farm Work	https://immi.homeaffairs.gov.au/what-we-do/whm-program/specified-work-conditions/specified-work-462.
Eligible 417 Farm Work	https://immi.homeaffairs.gov.au/visas/getting-a-visa/visa-listing/work-holiday-417/specified-work
2nd Work Holiday 462 Application	https://immi.homeaffairs.gov.au/visas/getting-a-visa/visa-listing/work-holiday-462/second-work-holiday-462
2nd Work Holiday 417 Application	https://immi.homeaffairs.gov.au/visas/getting-a-visa/visa-listing/work-holiday-417/second-working-holiday-417
3rd Work Holiday 462 Application	https://immi.homeaffairs.gov.au/visas/getting-a-visa/visa-listing/work-holiday-462/third-work-and-holiday-462

3rd Work Holiday 417 Application	https://immi.homeaffairs.gov.au/visas/getting-a-visa/visa-listing/work-holiday-417/third-working-holiday-417
Sponsorship Visas	https://immi.homeaffairs.gov.au/visas/getting-a-visa/visa-listing/temporary-skill-shortage-482
Fruit Picking Guidebook	https://www.amazon.com/fruit-picking-guide-Australia-2020/dp/1655588095/ref=sr_1_7?dchild=1&keywords=budget+travel+australia&qid=1606199021&s=books&sr=1-7

The Statement: I thrive and enjoy my Australian life.

My hope for you is that you have direction, excitement, and a foundation of tools to succeed in your move to Australia with a working holiday visa. Now you can wing it as much as you want because you have all the important knowledge you need to succeed in your move.

There are so many unknown possibilities and beautiful places to see and experience that are just a visa away.

Buy the ticket. Don't worry about all the little technical things. Because, with this book, and you believing in yourself, you will do it. If I could go back to the first day I landed in Oz, mind you, my bags got left in LA and it was kind of a fiasco, I wish someone had told me at least one point in this book. It would have lifted some kind of weight and pressure off of my shoulders. But, I am so happy I am able to share all of this with you now. You have a certain amount of years, why not spend (at least) one of them in Australia?

You are now ready to F*ck off to Australia!

App Checklist

These apps will be helpful before and during your time in Australia. Make a folder in your phone to keep it all organised. Some have already been mentioned throughout the book and some are new.

Transportation

QLD - Translink/GoCard	https://translink.com.au/plan-your-journey/mytranslink
WA - TransPerth	https://www.transperth.wa.gov.au/App
SA - MetroCard	https://mc.adelaidemetro.com.au
TAS - GreenCard	https://www.metrotas.com.au/communication/apps/
ACT - MyWay *there is not an app, but a website*	https://form.act.gov.au/smartforms/landing.htm?formCode=1009-myway
VIC - Myki	https://www.ptv.vic.gov.au/footer/about-ptv/digital-tools-and-updates/mobile-apps/
NSW - Opal	https://transportnsw.info/apps/opal-travel
NT - Tap &Ride *there is not an app, but a website*	https://nt.gov.au/driving/public-transport-cycling/public-buses/nt-bus-tracker-app
Rome 2 Rio ***Directions to and from anywhere in the world***	https://www.rome2rio.com/about/rome2rio-app/

Hopper	https://www.hopper.com
JetStar	https://www.jetstar.com/au/en/jetstar-app
Qantas	https://www.qantas.com/au/en/qantas-experience/qantas-app.html

Finance

ANZ	https://www.anz.com.au/ways-to-bank/mobile-banking-apps/anz-app/
Commonwealth	https://www.commbank.com.au/digital-banking/commbank-app.html
Westpac	https://www.westpac.com.au/personal-banking/online-banking/ways-to-bank/mobile-banking/
Raiz *investing app that rounds up your change from your transactions linked through your credit card*	https://raizinvest.com.au
XE *currency exchange*	https://www.xe.com

The Happiest Hour *finds the best specials at pubs and restaurants in your vicinity*	https://thehappiesthour.com
Trail Wallet *keep track of your expenses and create a budget*	https://voyagetravelapps.com/trail-wallet/

Accommodation

Hostelworld	https://www.hostelworld.com/mobile-app?source=ppc_gooads_brand_dsk_search_brd_en_oceania&_branch_match_id=860365343057064586
Couchsurfing	https://about.couchsurfing.com/about/mobile/
AirBnb	https://www.airbnb.com.au/mobile
Flatmates	https://apps.apple.com/us/app/flatmates/id1489897686
	https://play.google.com/store/apps/details?id=au.com.reagroup.flatmates&hl=en

Measurements

1 Liter = .26 gallons
1/2 liter = 1.05 pints
1 Meter = 3.3 feet
Centimeter = 2/5 of an inch
Kilometer = 6/10 of a mile
Kilogram (kilo) = 2.2 pounds

The formula for converting Fahrenheit to Celsius is: (__°C x 9/5) + 32 = __°F). But remembering these key temperatures will give you an idea of what each temperature feels like.

0°C = 32°F
5°C = 41°F
10°C = 50°F
15°C = 59°F
20°C = 68°F
25°C = 77°F
30°C = 86°F
35°C = 95°F
40°C = 104°F
45°C = 113°F

Random Aussie Facts & Info

Tipping is not custom in Australia: you tip if you feel like the service was extra special.

The correct way to eat Vegemite toast is: one piece of toast, a lot of butter and about half a teaspoon spread of Vegemite.

Any red and white fishing lure in Australia is referred to as a "Qantas".

Thursday Island, part of the Torres Strait Islands at the very top of Australia, has one of the nicest hospitals that you could ever be admitted into.

Swim between the flags…

Unless you have already accepted that you are going to be a wrinkly old woman or a wrinkly old man who can defy sun cancer, wear sunscreen every day. You are not tougher than the sun. Especially the Australian sun.

You are going to need a "Type I" charger for outlets, it is in the shape of a "V"

This will save you time at the self-checkout line in Coles: Bell Peppers = Capsicums, Cilantro = Coriander, Arugula = Rocket and Napkins = Soviets

Your Pre - Oz Weekly Assignment!

This is for you to get more excited! Its only boring if you think it's boring, so you make it as fun as you want!

Each week before the day you are set to step on the plane to Australia, you will:

- Research a person, place or thing
- Listen to a podcast or music
- Read articles, books, or posts
- Watch films or YouTube videos

All about something you do not know already about Australia. It can be anything your heart desires! Some examples are:

- Famous Australians
- Current Events
- Types of food
- Historical background
- Finance/Business
- Fashion Icons
- Geography/Terrain
- Musicians/Films
- Political figures
- Animals

Don't forget to throw an Aussie inspired party before you leave!

It can be anything in this world, but it has to relate to Oz. This could give you more insight on where you want to live, what you want to do, and what you want to learn when you enter the country.

Acknowledgements

Thank you, Luke Watkins of Wales, who inspired the title of this book with his famous tweet in 2018:

"Might f*ck off to Australia and get a job at a waterpark giving the nod to go down the slides."

Thank you, Candice Parry, Courtney Dean, Tasha Turner, Sam Turner, Anna Turner and Roy Turner, for giving me advice, helping me with edits and hearing me talk about it all the time.

And thank you, Jack and Fran of Back 2 Basics Adventures (@b2badventures) for the idea of the audio portion that you can listen to at: @mightfo2australia.

Thank you forever.

Cheers,
Carly

Might F*ck off to Australia is a Cardotti Classic.

For further questions or comments, please email
carlymurden@icloud.com

I am here to help.

Share this book so we can help more people f*ck off to Australia!

@mightfo2australia #cardotticlassic
#mfo2australia

Printed in Great Britain
by Amazon

21415112R00060